A Year in Barrowswold Forest

Written by Chris
Illustrated by Timo C

Contents

Collins

Starting Forest School

This year, our class is going to Forest School! This means we go to the forest one morning each week, to learn about the natural world by being in it and having fun. After register, we all get our wellies and coats and walk up the hill to Barrowswold Forest.

Round the camp fire

Debbie and Pete run Forest School. On our first day, they made a camp fire, and we sat on the circle of logs around it. We talked about the rules. There aren't many of them!

Rules of Forest School

- Don't go near the fire without a grown-up.
- Don't go out of the site without a grown-up.
- Don't climb on the fence.
- Be respectful to the animals and plants.
- Look after each other. ← Debbie says these are
- Have fun! ← the most important rules of all!

Choosing what to do

We all thought Pete and Debbie would tell us what they wanted us to do. But they said we could choose! We all wanted to explore, to play hide-and-seek and **Capture the Flag**, and things like that. The site has a pond and a stream, and trees to climb. There's a tool box and stashes of rope and **tarpaulins** and other things to play with. So there's lots to do!

tarpaulin

tree climbing

making a shelter

pond dipping

Bark rubbings

There are lots of different trees – it's a forest! We got some paper and wax crayons and did some rubbings of the tree **bark**. Different kinds of trees have different patterns. Pete told us the names of the different trees.

There's lots of nature in the forest, and we talked about how it'll change during the year. We got the idea of keeping this **scrapbook** to help us remember this year.

oak

cherry

sycamore

Autumn

The climbing tree

There's a great tree to climb on. It fell down in a storm one time, and now it's lying on its side. It's easy to get on it at the end where the roots are, and then you can climb along. You can get high up into the branches, if you're good at climbing.

bird's nest

fungus

roots

branches

ivy

Moss and fungus

There's moss on the parts of the tree we don't climb, and for a while there was a thing that looked like an ear – a jelly ear fungus. Debbie says most of the fungus is inside the tree, feeding on the dead wood.

jelly ear fungus

bracket fungus

electrified cat's tail moss

ordinary moss (that's really what it's called!)

honey fungus

Many of the smaller branches have fallen off now, and are rotting away on the ground. Sometimes the bark is coming off and under it you might see white threads: that's more of the fungus.

7

Rotten wood and minibeasts

Fungus is one of the first things to start **recycling** dead wood. Once the fungus has fed on dead wood for a while, water and minibeasts can get in.

When we were collecting sticks for the camp fire, we found some really rotten wood – it's spongy and falls to bits easily, and it's full of minibeasts like woodlice and centipedes. In the end, the rotten wood falls apart completely and becomes part of the soil in which more things grow.

woodlice

Acorns

We had a competition to collect the most acorns.
We saw a squirrel and a jay collecting acorns too.
Pete says a big oak tree can produce over a thousand
acorns every year – more in
some years. But most of them
get eaten and don't grow
into trees. That's probably
why the tree has to
make so many.

jay

squirrel

Autumn leaves

Many of the trees are dropping their leaves now.
Pete says trees that have big leaves can't keep them in
the winter – the leaves would freeze and die. So the tree
gets rid of them. That means there are lots of fallen
leaves to play in!

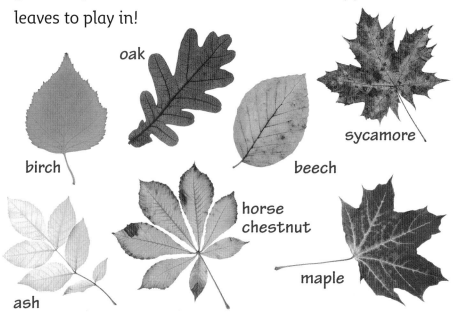

oak

sycamore

birch

beech

horse
chestnut

maple

ash

Trees don't all lose their leaves though
– some are called "evergreens"
because they don't! These have
tough leaves like needles,
which don't get damaged by
the winter frosts.

Leaf mobiles

We dipped some leaves in melted beeswax and hung them on string to make hanging mobiles. The wax goes hard again when it cools and it stops the leaves from falling to bits.

Winter is coming

We saw birds eating the blackberries. They know winter's coming! Plants need light and warmth to grow, so during the winter lots of plants die or stop growing. Many minibeasts die in autumn and winter too. Fewer plants and minibeasts means there's less food for many animals in winter. It's a hard time for lots of creatures!

Animals in autumn

Debbie says animals can tell that the winter is coming, because the days are getting shorter and it's getting cooler.

house martin

When we walk to Forest School, we can see birds coming together on the phone lines. Some are swallows and house martins – they eat insects, and there won't be many here in the winter. So they're getting ready to fly to Africa. But they'll come back in spring.

swallow

House martins have a short forked tail; swallows have much longer forked tails.

Hedgehogs go to sleep in the winter because there isn't much food. This is called "hibernating".

We made this home for a hedgehog to hibernate in!

Plants in autumn

Lots of plants have made seeds now. It's best for the plant if its seeds don't grow right next to it, using up the same sunshine and water. So the wind works to scatter the seeds. Animals can do this too, by carrying the seeds away to eat them.

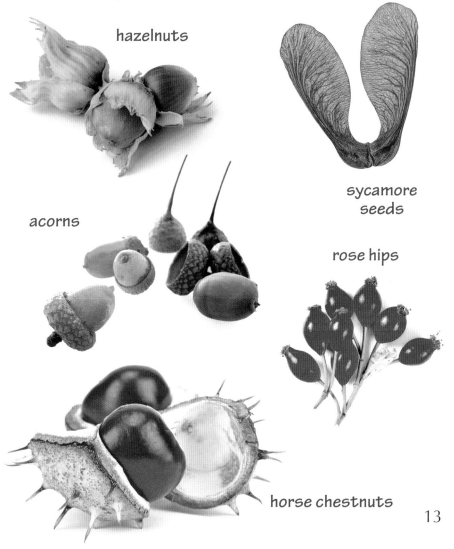

hazelnuts

sycamore seeds

acorns

rose hips

horse chestnuts

13

Winter

Making charcoal

Debbie asked if we wanted
to make some charcoal.
We gathered some little sticks –
Debbie says that hazel,
elder or willow is best.
That made things easy
because there's a big
willow tree down by
the stream.

14

Debbie put our willow sticks into an old metal biscuit tin. She made some holes in the lid, and put it on the fire. After a while, smoke came out of the holes. Then Debbie took the tin off the fire and let it cool.

The sticks had gone silver-black and a bit shiny. Charcoal is all soft – you can draw with it, or rub it on your face and hands for camouflage. Nobody minds if you get dirty at Forest School!

Ice is nice

It rained, and now it's freezing. But that doesn't stop us going to Forest School. You just have to remember warm clothes!

The trees are mostly bare now. We made some ice ornaments for them, by putting some water in those silver cases that hold little pies or cakes.

Then we put some leaves, twigs and berries in, and left a length of string dangling over the side.

We left them at Forest School overnight and hoped they'd freeze.

Our teacher took us on a special trip to Forest School at lunchtime the next day to hang the ornaments up in a tree. They had frozen solid in the night. Now they look like Christmas decorations!

Next week, our decorations had melted. There was still ice on the pond. Probably the decorations melted because they were little and were hanging up in the winter sunshine. But when we broke the ice on the pond, we could see it was thick, so it takes longer to melt.

Animal tracks

We could see some animal tracks in the frozen mud.
Pete could tell us about the tracks – we found tracks of
roe deer and a fox! Roe deer
have little hooves, but
a fox has paws like
a small dog.

fox tracks

roe deer tracks

Pete had some plaster of Paris and showed us how to take casts of a track mark.

Here's how we did it!

Making a plaster cast

- Make a strip of cardboard into a ring a bit bigger than the track mark.

- Push the ring into the mud over the track mark.

- Mix plaster of Paris with water.

- Pour the plaster into the cardboard ring.

- Wait until the plaster is dry and hard.

- Pick up the plaster. It has a bump in the shape of the track mark!

Animals in winter

Squirrels come to the bird feeders we made.
So do many different kinds of birds. It must
be harder for them
to find food now.
There aren't many
berries, seeds or
minibeasts left.

Plants in winter

All the leaves are down now and are rotting away.
The **undergrowth** has died away too – you can go right
through the bit that's usually the **nettle** patch.

You can see the shapes of the trees very clearly
without their leaves. The trees don't grow in this cold
season with its short days – they're waiting for spring.
Sometimes you can see birds' nests in the branches.

When it was windy,
a bird's nest blew
down, so we could
take a closer look
at it.

Spring

Everything's growing

Now it's spring, it's warmer and there's more light. The plants on the forest floor have started growing quickly. More plants means more food for animals, so lots of things start to happen in the forest.

The swallows and house martins are coming back, now there are flying insects for them to catch and eat again. We've also spotted some baby animals. The sheep in the field have lambs now, and one day we saw a baby rabbit!

A mystery track

We found a clear track that goes straight under the fence. Some hair or fur had got caught on the wire.

We could see some little holes scratched into the mud nearby, and one bigger hole that had some dung in it. It didn't look like sheep dung. So those were our clues – what kind of creature has short grey hairs, and makes holes like that?

Mystery solved!

Today, we followed the mysterious track in the other direction, away from the fence. In one place, there was some soft mud and we saw a footprint. It looked too big to be a squirrel, and not like a rabbit or dog's footprint.

The track led to a big hole going steeply down into the bank. We didn't poke anything into the hole or go too close – we didn't know what was inside! We could see that something had been digging quite recently, throwing some loose soil out into a heap near the hole.

We showed Pete the track and the hole. He said we'd found the badger's hole, which is called a "sett".

we asked Pete about the badgers. He said that they
are shy and that they come out at night. So we're
never going to see them. But Debbie knew all about
the badgers, because she stayed up once and took some
photos of them!

Badger food

Badgers eat mostly earthworms, which they dig out of little holes called "snuffle holes", like the ones we saw in the field. But badgers also eat other small animals (like rabbits or hedgehogs) as well as bulbs and berries.

We drew this picture, called a food web. It shows what badgers eat.

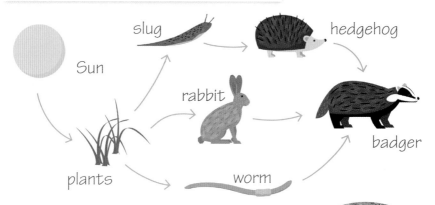

Badger families

A badger family can live in the same sett for years and years. That's why the tracks that they make become so clear. We could see a short track down the side of the bank that had gone very smooth – Debbie said the badgers use this as a slide to play on!

27

Animals in spring

Animal babies

Summer is the best time to be a baby animal growing up, because there's more food. So lots of animals have babies in spring.

We saw some frogs' eggs in the pond, and then a week or two later we could see tadpoles.

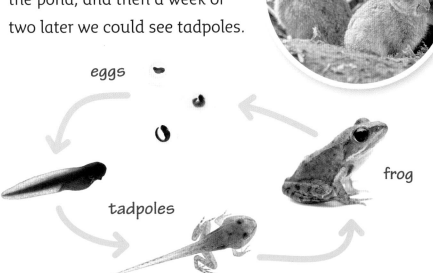

eggs

tadpoles

frog

Once, when we moved a big piece of bark, we saw an adult frog! It was quite hard to see, and we only noticed when it hopped away.

Birds

In spring, the birds sing more than in winter. Sometimes we can see birds flying along with straw or sticks, which they must be using to make nests.

In April, we heard a cuckoo. This bird flies here from Africa each spring. Its call really does sound like someone saying "cuckoo"!

Plants in spring

Tree flowers

Trees that lost their leaves in the autumn are growing new leaves from buds. Some of the trees grow flowers, and most of them don't look like garden flowers! Birch trees have flowers called catkins, which look like cats' tails.

birch

hazel

field maple

oak

cherry

hawthorn

Flowers from bulbs

Things start to grow on the forest floor. Flowers like snowdrops and bluebells grow from bulbs under the ground. Pete says that the woodland flowers need to grow quickly, before the trees are covered in leaves and the forest

floor is all in shade. The bulbs are full of energy stored from last year and they help the plants grow quickly – unless a badger eats the bulb, of course (badgers like bluebell bulbs!).

Some plants, like the ferns by the stream, don't have flowers at all.

31

Summer

Squirrels and shelters

It's summer – and it's raining. We had fun making dens, though. We made one from sticks, propping them up against each other like a **tipi**.

A squirrel had made a nest – a "drey" – high in a tree near where we were building. It was also made out of twigs. In summer, the squirrels make dreys that are quite **flimsy**. The squirrels make their winter dreys much thicker so as to keep out the cold.

We also made a shelter with a tarpaulin – a waterproof cloth – which we tied on to trees to make a roof.

If we really had to survive in the woods, we'd need to make a shelter, and find things to eat. We'd also need to find water that we could drink – maybe you could drink the rain, but the forecast is for some hot dry weather.

If you were surviving in the woods, you wouldn't want to drink the water from the stream and the pond – it can be muddy and can have bits in it.

Filtering water

We tried using an old sock to filter the water – that was something we read about in a survival book. We got a bucket of water from the stream and tipped some of it through the sock and into a jar. The sock worked quite well – the water was less muddy when it had been through the sock, and the sock got dirty.

dirty water

sock

jar

cleaner water

But Pete said we still shouldn't drink the water – it could have germs in it, because they are too small to get stuck in the sock. Pete said that we could boil the water to kill the germs. But even so, it's safer to drink tap water!

Solar still

We tried another way of getting water that we could drink if we had to live in the forest – we made a **solar still**.

Making a solar still

- We dug a little hole in a sunny spot.

- We put a bowl of muddy water inside, and stood a mug in the bowl.

- Then we covered the hole with a piece of clear plastic, and put a little stone just above the mug.

As the sun shone down, first the inside of the plastic got wet. That was because it was getting hot inside the hole, and the water was **evaporating** into **water vapour** – which is like steam but cooler. But the water vapour couldn't get past the plastic, so water began to drip into the mug.

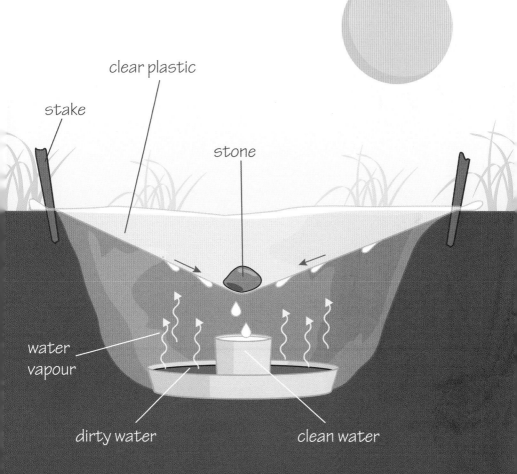

clear plastic

stake

stone

water
vapour

dirty water

clean water

Drips and drops

Our solar still was working, but it was collecting clean water very slowly. Pete said he'd look after it for us, and when we went back to Forest School, it had collected more water. The water that had collected in the mug wasn't muddy at all – all of the mud had stayed in the bowl. So it does work, but it's very slow, and it wouldn't work well on cloudy days because it needs the heat of the sun.

A forest greenhouse

Pete had done something to show us – he'd tied a clear plastic bag over some of the leaves on a tree like a little greenhouse. Trees and other plants draw water up out of the soil and it comes out of the leaves as water vapour. If we were surviving in the forest, we could collect a little water this way too.

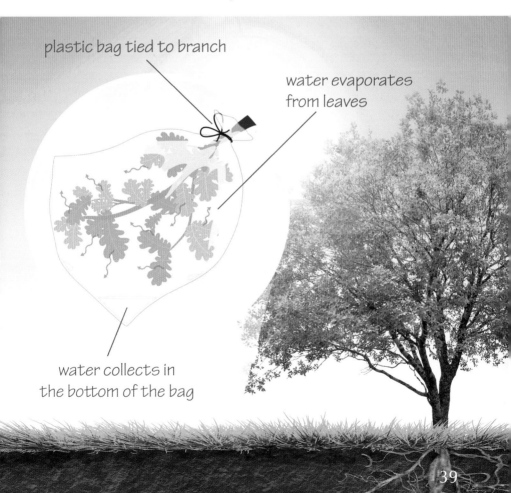

plastic bag tied to branch

water evaporates from leaves

water collects in the bottom of the bag

Animals in summer

There are some butterflies now in the **clearings**, and lots of minibeasts to find under old wood. There are even more minibeasts to find by dipping in the pond, like pond skaters and water snails.

orange tip butterfly

fritillary butterfly

woodlouse

millipede

water boatman

pond skater

Plants in summer

It can be hot in the forest in summer. But it's very shady under the beech trees – if you look up, you can see hardly any daylight, because the leaves are so packed together.

Pete says that leaves use sunlight to help the plant make food, and the beech leaves are close together so the tree can catch as much sunshine as possible.

Places to hide

The bluebells we saw in spring have died back now. Other things are growing very quickly – some of the undergrowth is very tall and good for hiding in when we play games. But brambles and nettles are growing quickly too, so we have to be careful of thorns and stings!

Goodbye, Forest School!

Today was our last day of Forest School – we wish we could come back next year, but it's the next class' turn. But we've made a bird feeder for our school, and we'll go back to the woods sometimes to play and to check up on the wildlife. That way, we'll be able to use the forest skills we've learnt.

We all said goodbye to Pete and Debbie. We'd made them a card and a cake. We all ate the cake and talked about what we're going to do in the summer holidays. After that, it'll be autumn again, and some new children will be coming to Barrowswold Forest School, and everything will be starting over again.

Glossary

bark	the tough material that covers the outside of a tree
Capture the Flag	an outdoor game where two teams each have a flag and try to capture the other team's flag
clearings	parts of a wood where there aren't many trees
evaporating	changing from a liquid into steam or vapour
flimsy	not very strong
nettle	a wild plant which have leaves covered with fine hairs that sting you
recycling	using something again
scrapbook	a book with empty pages in which you can stick things such as pictures so you can keep them.
solar still	a tool for using the sun's rays to get clean water from dirty water
tarpaulins	waterproof cloths used to make shelters
tipi	a round tent, first made by Native American peoples from animal skins or the outer covering of trees
undergrowth	bushes and plants growing together under the trees in a forest
water vapour	water that is turned into a gas, but isn't boiling hot

Index

Seasons in the forest

Spring

Winter

Summer

Autumn

 Ideas for reading

Written by Clare Dowdall, PhD
Lecturer and Primary Literacy Consultant

Reading objectives:
- read books that are structured in different ways
- discuss understanding and explain the meaning of words in context
- make predictions from details stated and implied
- retrieve and record information from non-fiction

Spoken language objectives:
- articulate and justify answers, arguments and opinions
- participate in discussions, presentations, performances, role play, improvisations and debates

Curriculum links: Living things and their habitats

Resources: sock, bowl, muddy water, chalk, crayons, paper

Build a context for reading

- Look at the front cover. Ask children to describe what they can see, and explain which season they think is shown, justifying their ideas.
- Read the blurb together. Talk about what Forest School is – from children's experiences or associations.
- Check that children are familiar with the names and order of the seasons, and some key phenomena associated with each one.

Understand and apply reading strategies

- Read pp2–3 together. Ask children if they agree with Debbie's choice of the most important rules, and why they think that these are the most important to her.
- Ask for a volunteer to read pp4–5. Look at the word "tarpaulins". Help children to use the contextual information to work out its meaning, then model how to check using the glossary.